THE STORY OF THE CLEVELAND CAVALIERS

Brad Daugherty

Jarrett Allen

A HISTORY OF HOOPS

THE STORY OF THE

CLEVELAND
CAVALIERS

JIM WHITING

Hot Rod Williams

CREATIVE EDUCATION / CREATIVE PAPERBACKS

Published by Creative Education and Creative Paperbacks
P.O. Box 227, Mankato, Minnesota 56002
Creative Education and Creative Paperbacks are imprints of
The Creative Company
www.thecreativecompany.us

Design and production by Blue Design (www.bluedes.com)
Art direction by Rita Marshall
Production layout by Rachel Klimpel and Ciara Beitlich

Photographs by Alamy (UPI), AP Images (Tony Dejak, Mark Duncan, J.P. Moczulski, Eric Risberg), Corbis, Getty (Al Bello, Mark Blinch, Nathaniel S. Butler, Diamond Images, Focus On Sport, David Liam Kyle, Manny Millan, Jason Miller, John Mottern, Doug Pensinger, Dick Raphael, Gregory Shamus, Sarah Stier, Tony Tomsic), Newscom (Ting Shen), Shutterstock (Brocreative, Valentin Valkov)

Library of Congress Cataloging-in-Publication Data
Names: Whiting, Jim, 1943- author.
Title: The story of the Cleveland Cavaliers / by Jim Whiting.
Description: Mankato, Minnesota : Creative Education | Creative Paperbacks, [2023] | Series: Creative Sports: A History of Hoops | Includes index. | Audience: Ages 8-12 | Audience: Grades 4-6 | Summary: "Middle grade basketball fans are introduced to the extraordinary history of NBA's Cleveland Cavs with a photo-laden narrative of their greatest successes and losses"-- Provided by publisher.
Identifiers: LCCN 2022007527 (print) | LCCN 2022007528 (ebook) | ISBN 9781640266223 (library binding) | ISBN 9781682771785 (paperback) | ISBN 9781640007635 (ebook)
Subjects: LCSH: Cleveland Cavaliers (Basketball team)--History--Juvenile literature.
Classification: LCC GV885.52.C57 W553 2023 (print) | LCC GV885.52.C57 (ebook) | DDC 796.323/640977132--dc23/eng/20220518
LC record available at https://lccn.loc.gov/2022007527
LC ebook record available at https://lccn.loc.gov/2022007528

Larry Nance

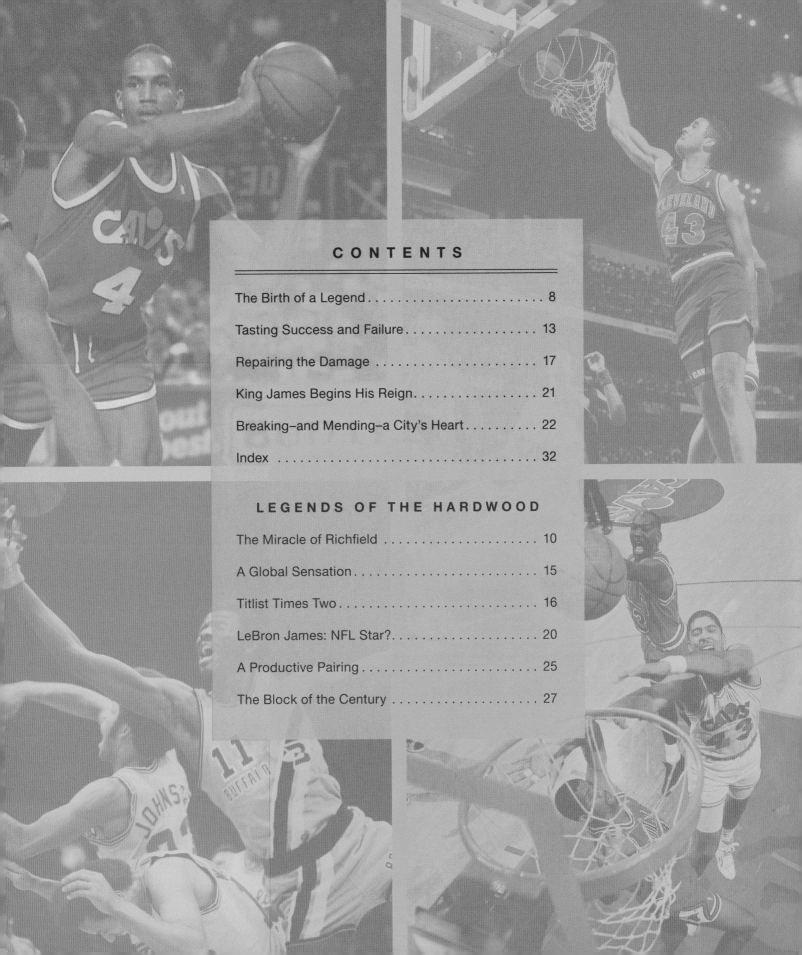

CONTENTS

LEGENDS OF THE HARDWOOD

THE BIRTH OF A LEGEND

On May 22, 2003, LeBron James signed a contract with the shoe and apparel giant Nike. It would pay him $90 million. James actually took a $25 million pay cut by signing with Nike. Reebok had offered him $115 million. James thought that Nike would make a better long-term partner. What makes these numbers especially eye-popping is that James was only 18 years old! He was still in high school. He had never played in a National Basketball Association (NBA) game.

James grew up in Akron, Ohio. He led his high school team to three state championships. Twice he was named Gatorade National Player of the Year. He was on the cover of Sports Illustrated when he was a junior.

LeBron James

LEGENDS
OF THE HARDWOOD

CLEVELAND VS. WASHINGTON
NBA PLAYOFFS
EASTERN CONFERENCE SEMIFINALS
APRIL 13–29, 1976

THE MIRACLE OF RICHFIELD

The Washington Bullets were heavily favored in the 1976 playoffs. That didn't matter to Cleveland fans. They were stoked about their team's first playoff appearance. "The fans would get rolling a half hour before the game," said Austin Carr. "They'd be stomping on the floor, 'Let's go, Cavs! Let's go, Cavs!' It was to the point where the entire building was shaking." The series was especially exciting because of how close the scores were. Two of the Cavs' first three victories were by a single point. Dick Snyder's jump shot with four seconds left in Game 7 gave Cleveland an 87–85 win. Fans rushed the floor and mobbed the players.

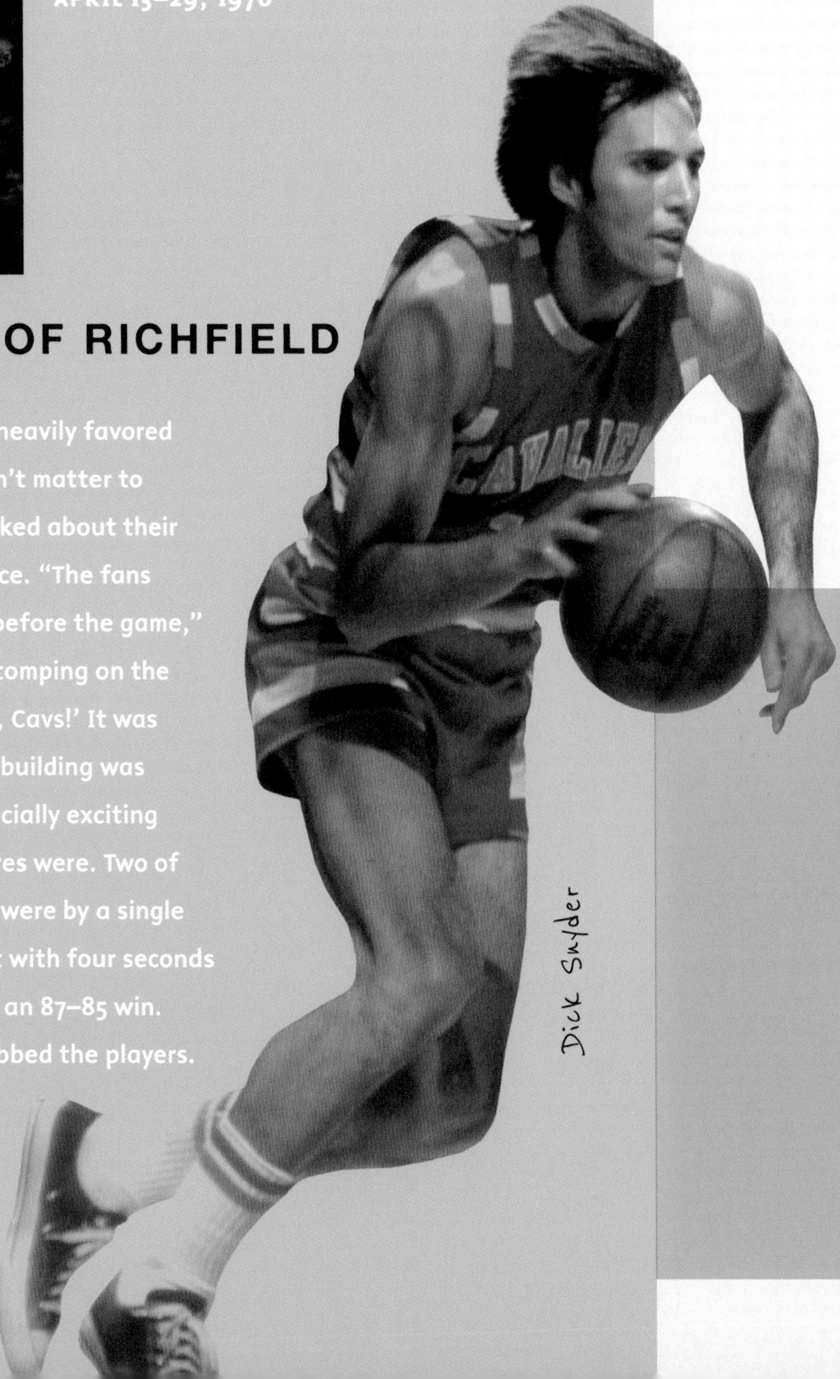

Dick Snyder

LeBron James

In a startling coincidence, the Cleveland Cavaliers won the draft lottery the same day James signed his endorsement with Nike. That gave them the first pick in the NBA Draft. There was no doubt that they would pick James. The young star made his debut with the Cavaliers on October 29 in a game against the Sacramento Kings. Not surprisingly, James was nervous. "I couldn't sleep the night before," he said. He was under a lot of pressure.

Fans had high expectations. Cleveland was desperate for a winner. The city's last pro sports title was in 1964 when the Browns won the National Football League (NFL) championship. Fans weren't the only ones with high expectations. James had to live up to his Nike contract.

James scored his first NBA points a minute and a half into the game with a baseline jumper. Late in the quarter, he stole the ball. He was on his way to the hoop for an easy dunk. He stopped and passed to Ricky Davis, who scored. James finished the quarter with 12 points, 3 assists, 2 rebounds and 2 steals. His final numbers were 25 points, 9 rebounds, 6 assists, and 4 steals. "Nobody knew exactly what LeBron was going to do," said Cavs coach Paul Silas. "I thought he was going to be good, but not nearly as good as he was. It was unbelievable." With James, the Cavaliers had the best chance to dominate in the league since the team's start in 1970.

TASTING SUCCESS AND FAILURE

Cleveland's NBA history dates back more than 50 years. The NBA league added teams in Portland, Buffalo, and Cleveland in 1970. Cleveland seemed like an odd choice. The city was going through hard times. But local businessman Nick Mileti believed in its future. He raised enough money to pay for the franchise. A Cleveland newspaper held a name-the-team contest. More than 11,000 people responded. Local resident Jerry Tomko submitted the winning entry. It was Cavaliers, often shortened to Cavs. He wrote, "They represent a group of daring, fearless men, whose life's pact was never surrender, no matter what the odds."

The odds were certainly against them in the first season. The Cavaliers consisted of veterans whom other teams didn't want and untried rookies. Coach Bill Fitch was realistic about their chances. "Remember, my name is Fitch, not [magician Harry] Houdini," he said. The Cavs lost their first 15 games. They edged out fellow expansion team Portland by two points for their first victory. Then they dropped another 12 in a row. They finished 15–67. It was the league's worst record.

Cleveland had the first pick in the 1971 NBA Draft. They took 6-foot-4 shooting guard Austin Carr. He became the face of the team. The Cavs won 23, 32, and 29 games the following three seasons. The losing records kept fans away. There was another problem. The team played its home games in the outdated Cleveland Arena. Mileti built a new arena in nearby Richfield in 1974. Many people criticized

Jim Chones

Mileti for the site. It was in the middle of a cornfield more than 20 miles from downtown Cleveland. The doubters were wrong. Home attendance doubled. The Cavs added sharpshooting guard Dick Snyder and towering forward Jim Chones for the 1974–75 season. They helped Cleveland finish 40–42. The team missed the playoffs by just one game.

Cleveland added veteran shot blocker and rebounder Nate Thurmond the following season. The Cavs went 49–33. They qualified for the playoffs for the first time. Fitch did his best Houdini imitation in the first round. Cleveland defeated the Washington Bullets, 4 games to 3. The series became known as "the Miracle of Richfield." Newspaper reporter Burt Graeff wrote, "The place was a frenzy…. That season is when basketball in Cleveland was born." Unfortunately, Chones broke his foot in practice before the next round. Cleveland played hard against the Boston Celtics. They lost the series, 4 games to 2.

Fitch guided the Cavs to 43–39 records the following two seasons, but there were no more miracles. The Cavs were bounced in the first round of the playoffs both times. They stumbled to a 30–52 mark in 1978–79. Fitch quit. The next five years were perhaps the low point of Cavaliers history. Bad management decisions plagued the team. Shooting guard World B. Free was one of the few bright spots. He joined the team in 1982. He became the leading scorer. "World sincerely believes every shot he takes will go in," said fellow guard John Bagley. "A lot of times, he's right."

The Cavs continued their losing ways in 1984–1985. They started 2–19 and finished at 36–46. Yet the record was good enough for a playoff berth. They lost to Boston in the first round, 3 games to 1. It was a heartbreaking series. All three losses were by three points or fewer.

WORLD B. FREE
SHOOTING GUARD
HEIGHT: 6-FOOT-2
CAVALIERS SEASONS:
1982–86

A GLOBAL SENSATION

Lloyd Free was a playground sensation while he was growing
up on Brooklyn, New York. His 44-inch vertical leap allowed
him to do moves such as a full 360-degree turn in mid-air
before dunking the ball. His friends were so impressed that
the titles "all-city" and "all-county" weren't good enough.
They called him "All-World" because he could hit shots
"around the world." They often shortened it to "World." The
nickname followed him through college and into the NBA.
Just before joining the Cavs, he legally changed his name
from Lloyd Free to World B. Free.

AND CAVALIERS

LEGENDS
OF THE HARDWOOD

IMAN SHUMPERT
SHOOTING GUARD
HEIGHT: 6-FOOT-5
CAVALIERS SEASONS:
2014–17

TITLIST TIMES TWO

Iman Shumpert averaged nearly seven points and three rebounds when he
was a Cav. He played important minutes off the bench as the team upset the
Golden State Warriors to win the 2016 NBA title. Five years later he was busting
moves on a different kind of floor: *Dancing with the Stars*. He and partner
Daniella Karagach overcame a slow start and judges' skepticism to become fan
favorites. They racked up perfect scores in the final. "Holy cow!" said judge
Carrie Ann Inaba when they finished. "That was genius!" Shumpert is the first
NBA player to win the Mirror Ball Trophy on *Dancing with the Stars*. He is the
only person to achieve this unique double set of championships.

Lenny Wilkens

REPAIRING THE DAMAGE

After two more losing seasons, former player Lenny Wilkens became coach. He led the Cavs to a winning record in 1987–88, going 42–40. They had drafted 7-foot center Brad Daugherty and explosive guard Ron Harper the previous year. They added sharpshooting point guard Mark Price and long-limbed power forward Larry Nance. But Cleveland lost to Chicago in the first round of the playoffs.

Everything meshed the following year. The Cavs went 57–25. It was their best record. Once again, they couldn't get past Chicago in the playoffs. Injuries and bad trades led to losing records the next two seasons. The Cavs bounced back in 1991–92, winning 57 games again. But they lost to the Bulls in the Eastern Conference finals, 4 games to 2. When the Bulls bounced the Cavs from the playoffs yet again in 1992–93, Wilkens was done. "It's been a great seven years with the Cavaliers," he said. "However, I think it's time to move on." Defensive-minded Mike Fratello replaced him. "I'd rather win ugly than lose pretty," said the new coach. Ugly or not, the team kept winning for several more seasons. But Cleveland still made early playoff exits.

Vitaly Potapenko

The Cavs missed out on a golden opportunity in the 1996 NBA Draft. Shooting guard Kobe Bryant declared for the Draft immediately after a spectacular high school career. He was still on the board when it was Cleveland's turn. Cleveland chose 6-foot-10 center Vitaly Potapenko instead. He seemed like a better pick with an average of more than 20 points and 7 rebounds a game in college. His field goal shooting percentage was an impressive 60 percent. But the "Ukraine Train" never left the station. He lasted less than three seasons in Cleveland and averaged just seven points a game. Bryant became one of the greatest players in NBA history.

A three-way trade brought power forward Shawn Kemp to Cleveland in 1997. He was a starter in the 1998 All-Star Game. The following year, he averaged more than 20 points. But injuries, constant coaching changes, and roster turnovers hounded the team. The Cavs of the early 2000s often appeared to be playing street ball. They sported a flashy style but lacked teamwork.

Shawn Kemp

19

LEBRON JAMES

POWER/SMALL FORWARD

HEIGHT: 6-FOOT-8

CAVALIERS SEASONS:

2003–10, 2014–18

LEBRON JAMES: NFL STAR?

LeBron James played wide receiver for his high school football team for two years. He was named All-Ohio both times. Ohio State and Notre Dame wanted him to play football for them. Some people even think he could play in the NFL. "He's a 6-foot-8, 250-pound freak of stature," wrote ESPN's Tim Graham. "He would tower above NFL defensive backs and other receivers." During the NBA lockout in 2011, both Dallas and Seattle offered him a contract. "It definitely got my blood flowing again, my mind racing again about the game of football," he said. When the lockout ended, so did the possibility of James playing on Sundays. He did make a brief appearance in the Madden NFL 12 video game released that year.

KING JAMES BEGINS HIS REIGN

Cleveland bottomed out in 2002–03 with a 17–65 record. It was the team's worst mark in 21 years. The dismal showing gave the Cavs the opportunity to draft James. He proved that his first game wasn't a fluke. Later that season, he became the youngest player in NBA history to score at least 40 points. He was just the third rookie to average at least 20 points, 5 rebounds, and 5 assists. Not surprisingly, he was selected NBA Rookie of the Year. He helped Cleveland win 35 games, doubling its record from the year before. In the previous season, average attendance was 11,497. It rose to 18,288 as fans turned out in droves to watch James. He was even better in 2004–05. He averaged 27.2 points, 7.4 rebounds, 7.2 assists, and 2.2 steals per game. He became the youngest player named to the All-NBA Team. Cleveland narrowly missed the playoffs, finishing 42–40.

Quicken Loans founder Dan Gilbert bought the team before the 2005–06 season. "We believe it will be a golden era of basketball for the fans and community of this hardworking and well-deserving town," he said. That "golden era" got off to a good start. The Cavs won 50 games. The first round of the playoffs echoed the Miracle of Richfield. Cleveland beat the Washington Wizards by a point in two overtime games to win the series, 4–2. But it lost to Detroit in the next round. In 2006–07, the Cavs played in the NBA Finals for the first time. However, San Antonio proved too tough and the Spurs swept the series.

Cleveland advanced to the conference semifinals the following year. Boston bounced them. James had a sensational season in 2008–09. He averaged 28.4 points, 7.6 rebounds, and 7.2 assists per game. He earned his first Most Valuable Player (MVP) award. Cleveland had a franchise-record 66 wins. The Cavs swept both Detroit and Atlanta in the playoffs. But they lost the Eastern Conference finals to Orlando. James repeated as MVP the following year. When the Cavs lost in the conference semifinals, he was booed.

BREAKING—AND MENDING— A CITY'S HEART

After the 2010 season, James became a free agent. That meant he could sign with any team. He announced his choice in a TV show called *The Decision*. The program raised $6 million for charity. But there was no charity for Cleveland fans. James said he was joining the Miami Heat. He immediately became one of the most disliked athletes in the country. Gilbert published an open letter criticizing James. Fans burned his jersey.

Without James, the Cavs scraped together just 19 wins in the 2010–11 season. However, they struck gold in the NBA Draft for the second time in less than a decade. They used the top overall pick on point guard Kyrie Irving. Irving became an instant sensation. He averaged 18.5 points and 5.4 assists per game. He was named Rookie of the Year. Cleveland still struggled. The team won just 21 games in the lockout-shortened 2011–12 season, then 24 and 33 the following two seasons.

Everything changed on July 11, 2014. Two weeks earlier, James had become a free agent again. Where would he go this time? "What's most important for me is bringing one trophy back to Northeast Ohio," he told Sports Illustrated. "My relationship with Northeast Ohio is bigger than basketball. I didn't realize that four years ago. I do now."

Fans immediately forgave him. James jerseys were the top-selling NBA shirt that year. As a bonus, James persuaded power forward/center Kevin Love to join him in Cleveland. The rejuvenated Cavs fought their way to a 53–29 record. They swept both Boston and Atlanta in the playoffs. They blasted into the NBA Finals. But the Golden State Warriors won the series, 4 games to 2.

Kevin Love

KYRIE IRVING

POINT GUARD

HEIGHT: 6-FOOT-2

CAVALIERS SEASONS:

2011–17

A PRODUCTIVE PAIRING

Kyrie Irving was the country's second-ranked high school player in
2010. He announced his college choice on a national cable channel.
It was Duke University. Due to an injury, he played just 11 games
for the Blue Devils. That didn't matter to Cleveland. They made
him the first overall pick in the draft. He averaged more than 18
points and 5 assists every game. He was named NBA Rookie of the
Year. When LeBron James returned to Cleveland, the two of them
sparked the team to three straight NBA Finals. Irving is a member
of the Standing Rock Sioux Tribe. In 2018, the tribe gave him the
name Hela. It means "Little Mountain."

CLEVELAND CAVALIERS

With 57 wins in 2015–16, the Cavs charged into the playoffs. Easy series wins over Detroit, Atlanta, and Toronto propelled them into the Finals against Golden State again. The Warriors won an all-time best 73 games during the regular season. Point guard Steph Curry was the first unanimous MVP in league history. Golden State won three of the first four games. People thought Cleveland was finished. No team had ever come back from a 3–1 series deficit in the Finals. Even worse, Game 5 was at Golden State. The Warriors had lost only three times at home. For Cleveland sports fans, it looked like yet another disappointment.

Someone forgot to tell the Cavs that their season was over. They won the next two games. The series-deciding Game 7 went back and forth. With less than a minute left, the score was tied 89–89. Irving drained a three-point shot. Curry missed a three-pointer. With only a few seconds remaining, James sank a free throw. The Cavaliers were champs! James fell to the floor and wept for joy. "For us to be able to end this, end this drought, our fans deserve it," James said. "I came back to bring a championship to our city." He was the unanimous Finals MVP.

Cleveland faced off with the Warriors in the Finals in the next two seasons. It was no contest both times. Cleveland won just one game in 2016–17. They were swept the following season. James became a free agent again. He signed with the Los Angeles Lakers.

CLEVELAND VS. GOLDEN STATE
NBA FINALS
GAME 7
JUNE 19, 2016

CLEVELAND CAVALIERS

THE BLOCK OF THE CENTURY

Less than two minutes remained. The score was 89–89. Kyrie Irving went up for a shot. He missed. Warriors small forward Andre Iguodala grabbed the rebound. He streaked downcourt. He passed to Steph Curry. Curry passed it right back. Iguodala went up for what seemed to be an easy lay-in. It would give the Warriors the lead and thundering cheers from the home crowd. Moments earlier, LeBron James had been standing on the three-point line on the other side of the basket. Seemingly out of nowhere, he blocked the shot from behind. That preserved the tie and set up the frantic final moments that resulted in the Cavs win. "That block may go down as the single best play in James's entire career," said basketball researcher Kirk Goldsberry.

Evan Mobley

Without James, Cleveland plummeted to the bottom of the league standings for the next three years. Things started to turn around in the 2021–22 season. The team drafted power forward Evan Mobley. They re-signed dynamic center Jarrett Allen, who had averaged more than 10 rebounds per game in his two previous years. Third-year shooting/point guard Darius Garland showed steady improvement. Love provided veteran leadership. "For the first time since losing LeBron James to the Los Angeles Lakers, the Cavs have a direction for the franchise," said Ben Cooper of CavsNation. "They have built a solid young core that could become elite in the future."

Cleveland made a big acquisition before the 2022-23 season. They traded for three-time All-Star Donovan Mitchell. The former Utah Jazz guard has averaged nearly 24 points per game over his first five seasons in the league.

Cleveland fans have loyally supported the Cavs through all their ups and downs. They rejoiced when native son LeBron James led the team to its first-ever NBA title. They look forward to more championship banners hanging inside Rocket Mortgage FieldHouse.

Darius Garland

INDEX

Mark Price